My First Book of Vietnamese Words

An ABC Rhyming Book of Vietnamese Language and Culture

by Tran Thi Minh Phuoc
Illustrated by Nguyen Thi Hop and Nguyen Dong

TUTTLE Publishing

Tokyo | Rutland, Vermont | Singapore

Dedication

In memory of my loving parents Trần Minh Ý and Nguyễn Thị Sua.
To my family with love, respect, and laughter.
To the late Stephen Michael Jadick—this one's for you.
And to all the girls and boys who have never read about Việt Nam.
—Trần Thị Minh Phước

To our daughter Danchi, whose first Vietnamese words
brought joy to our hearts and inspired us.
—Nguyễn Thị Hợp & Nguyễn Đồng.

A Note to Parents

Vietnamese *(Tiếng Việt or Quốc Ngữ)* is the national and official language of Vietnam. Each word is monosyllabic. Multiple words can be combined to convey any part of speech. For example, the words *"sở thú"* together mean "zoo." Westerners generally combine two words/syllables into a single word when writing place names, such as Vietnam, *(Việt Nam)*, Saigon *(Sài Gòn)* and so on.

Unlike many other Asian languages, Vietnamese uses the alphabet of Romance languages, the difference lying in the diacritics that change the sound and meaning of the vowels. There are in fact 18 ways to write the vowels a and o, 12 to write e and u, and 6 to write i and y. **For a more in-depth look at Vietnamese vowels and language rules, and to hear the Vietnamese words in this book spoken aloud, please visit this book's page at www.tuttlepublishing.com.**

The letters f, j, w, and z do not exist in Vietnamese. Even so, there are 29 letters in the Vietnamese alphabet : *a*, *ă*, *â*, *b*, *c*, *d* (pronounced dz), *đ* (pronounced d as in English), *e*, *ê*, *g*, *h*, *i*, *k*, *l*, *m*, *n*, *o*, *ô*, *ơ*, *p*, *q*, *r*, *s*, *t*, *u*, *ư*, *v*, *x*, *y*.

Basic vowels are pronounced as follows:

a as in father
ă as in cat
â makes a short *u* sound, like in under
e as in tent
ê makes a long *a* sound, as in late
i makes a long *e* sound, as in me
o makes an *aw* sound as in law
ô as in so
ơ makes a *er/ur* sound, as in fur
u makes an *oo* sound as in moo
ư as in butter
y makes a long *e* sound, as in sheep (similar to *i*)

Most consonants are pronounced the same as in English. A few basic rules to remember are:

c is always hard, as in color
d makes a *dz* sound
đ makes the standard *d* sound
g is always hard as in garage
p is rarely found at the start of a word without being followed immediately
     by *h*. The *ph* diagraph makes an *f* sound, as it does in English. Words
     beginning with the *p* sound (like pyjama) are borrowed from French.
q is always followed by *u*, as in quick
s is pronounced *sh*, as in share
x is pronounced *s* as in son
y is treated as a vowel in Vietnamese

All Vietnamese words end in either *a*, *e*, *i*, *o*, *u*, *y*, *c*, *g*, *h*, *m*, *n*, *p* or *t*.

The culture of Vietnam is no less unique than the language, and many of the words chosen for this book are closely tied to Vietnamese foods, celebrations and values. We hope that this book will be the first of many explorations your child will make into this land and its people. Welcome, and have fun!

—Trần Thị Minh Phước

A is for **Ao**.
This is a **pond**
where kids chase the dragonflies
of which they are fond.

There's an old saying that if you let the dragonfly bite
your belly you'll be able to swim. Isn't that funny?

5

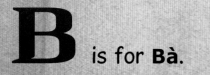

B is for **Bà**.
Our **grandma** loves to tell
us silly tales, that make us laugh.
She tells them very well!

In Vietnam children call
the dad's mother *bà nội*,
their mom's mother *bà ngoại*,
their dad's father, *ông nội* and their
mom's father *ông ngoại*.

6

C is for Cú.

The **owl** flies at night,
but when he hoots our grandma says
that something isn't right.

In Vietnam the hoot of an owl means
that bad luck or bad news is coming,
so no one likes to hear an owl.

7

D

D is for **Diều**.
On this cheery **kite**
a tiger is painted
in colors so bright.

The tiger is the third animal
in the Vietnamese zodiac. The other
animals are the Mouse, Water Buffalo, Cat,
Dragon, Snake, Horse, Goat, Monkey, Rooster,
Dog, and Pig.

8

E is for Én.

The **swallows** fly high,
soaring far, far away
through the bright blue sky.

Soup made from swallows' nests
is a special Vietnamese dish.

F is for **flute**.
The buffalo boy
plays the **sáo trúc**
with love and joy.

There is no letter F in the Vietnamese language,
but the *sáo trúc*, made of bamboo, is a traditional
flute that's often played at Vietnamese festivals.

G is for **Gừng**.
Tangy and yummy,
ginger root is
good for your tummy.

Ginger is used to soothe
the tummy in Vietnam
and lots of other places,
and it tastes good too!

H is for **Hồ**.

The **lake** deep and wide
is where lotus flowers grow
and sampans glide.

The beautiful lotus flower grows in muddy water and rises above the surface to bloom. A sampan is a flat-bottomed rowboat that is used a lot on Vietnam's rivers and lakes.

I is for Ít.

I is for **Ít.**
Filled with coconut
and mung bean
is a **rice flour ball**
in a banana leaf so green.

Bánh is the name of a kind of sweet treat
made in different shapes, sizes, and colors.
Bánh ít is a sweet rice flour ball wrapped
in banana leaf. Mung beans are a little like
lentils or peas and are really good for you!

13

J is for **juice**
that we drink right up!
We call it **nước ép**.
Won't you have a cup?

Vietnamese doesn't have a J sound but Vietnam has tasty juice from coconuts, mangoes, guavas, durians, and lots of other fruits.

14

K is for **Kẹo**.

This **candy** nice and sweet
is made from fruit called soursop.
It's a special New Year treat.

The soursop is a green, large, spiny,
tropical fruit with sweet seeded flesh.

L

L is for **Lụa**.
The **silk** we wear
is soft and pretty
and as light as air.

Vietnam has some of the most
beautiful silk in the world.

16

M is for **Mưa**.
The sweet cooling **rain**
feeds our crops and our flowers
(some goes down the drain).

In Vietnam the rainy season, called the monsoon
season, lasts from May to October.

17

N is for the **Nón**
that my mother weaves.
It's a cone-shaped **hat**
made of strong palm leaves.

Nón lá is a palm-leaf pointy hat that protects our heads from strong sun and wind.

18

O is for **Ông**.

To **grandpa** we say
"Long life, health and joy!"
He turned 80 today!

The 80th birthday is the most important
birthday for Vietnamese people. We
celebrate with a lot of brightly colored
decorations to bring luck and long life.

In Vietnam, women wear colorful pajamas on the streets and in the house. They are also called as ***đồ bộ***, which means "one set of same-colored clothing."

P is for **pyjama**.
What's this about?
Bright-colored **pajamas**
worn indoors or out.

20

Q is for **Quit.**

Tangerines are good for you
and bring good luck
the whole year through.

The tangerine is one of the five good
luck fruits we eat at New Year. The
other fruits are coconut, papaya,
mango, and soursop.

Children throw their bottom teeth on the roof and top teeth under the bed for the Tooth Mouse.

22

R is for **Răng**.
When you lose a **tooth** put it under your bed or up on the roof.

S is for **Sông**.

Shop keepers on the **river** sell fruit and fish and rice cakes as they float along together.

Vietnam is famous for its "floating markets"— boats that are like little shops on the river.

23

Chúc Mừng Năm Mới

T is for **Tết**.
Our **New Year** comes
with gongs and drums.
For flowers, we have
yellow mums.

Could you guess that *Tết* is the most important holiday of the year in Vietnam? The celebration lasts for days, and is filled with great food and lots of happy noise.

In Vietnam, little kids respect their older brothers and sisters, and older kids look after the little ones and keep them safe.

U

is for **Út**.
Who is brand-new?
The family's **youngest member**, that's who!

Crabs that live in the rice paddies
are a popular subject in the big
VietArt contest every year. Artists
love to draw and paint them.

V is for **Vẽ**.
The crabs my sister
draws
have big blue eyes
and bright red claws.

W is for **wisdom**.

Trí is what we say.
We grow wiser bit by bit,
more calm and thoughtful
day by day.

There is no letter W in the Vietnamese language, but wisdom is very important to the Vietnamese people. Other virtues like compassion *(nhân)*, rituals *(lễ)*, righteousness *(nghĩa)*, and trust *(tín)* are also important.

X is for **Xuân**.

Between January and
February
is the start of **spring**.
Birds fly home in a hurry.

In Vietnam and some other Asian countries the
seasons follow the phases of the moon. This is
called the Lunar Calendar. When it's mid-winter
in the West, it's spring in Vietnam.

Y

Y is for **Ý nguyện**.
Oh how I **wish**
for a big fried fish—
what a lucky New Year's dish!

Fish is one of the foods that bring good luck during *Tết*. At this time of year, we wish each other good health, good luck, and happiness.

29

Z

Z is for the **zoo** where animals stay. In the big **sở thú** they sleep and eat and play.

There is no letter Z in Vietnamese. The two words *sở* and *thú* are used together to express "zoo." Zoos in Vietnam have lions, tigers, elephants, monkeys, birds, and more, but no polar bears, seals, or zebras.

List of Words

Ao	Pond	**N**ón	Cone-shaped hat
Bà	Grandma	**Ô**ng	Grandpa
Cú	Owl	**P**yjama	Pajamas
Diều	Kite	**Q**uít	Tangerine
Én	Swallows	**R**ăng	Tooth
Flute **(Sáo trúc)**		**S**ông	River
Gừng	Ginger root	**T**ết	New Year
Hồ	Lake	**Ú**t	Youngest family member
Ít	Rice flour ball	**V**ẽ	Draw
Juice **(Nước ép)**		**W**isdom **(Trí)**	
Kẹo	Soursop candy	**X**uân	Spring
Lụa	Silk	**Ý** nguyện	Wish
Mưa	Rain	**Z**oo **(Sở thú)**	

Published by Tuttle Publishing, an imprint of Periplus Editions (HK) Ltd.

www.tuttlepublishing.com

Text and Illustrations ©2017 Periplus Editions (HK) Ltd

Library of Congress Control Number: 2016961922

ISBN 978-0-8048-4907-4

Distributed by

North America, Latin America & Europe
Tuttle Publishing, 364 Innovation Drive
North Clarendon, VT 05759-9436 U.S.A.
Tel: 1 (802) 773-8930
Fax: 1 (802) 773-6993
info@tuttlepublishing.com
www.tuttlepublishing.com

Japan
Tuttle Publishing, Yaekari Building, 3rd Floor,
5-4-12 Osaki, Shinagawa-ku, Tokyo 141 0032
Tel: (81) 3 5437-0171
Fax: (81) 3 5437-0755
sales@tuttle.co.jp
www.tuttle.co.jp

Asia Pacific
Berkeley Books Pte. Ltd., 61 Tai Seng Avenue #02-12,
Singapore 534167
Tel: (65) 6280-1330
Fax: (65) 6280-6290
inquiries@periplus.com.sg
www.periplus.com

Indonesia
PT Java Books Indonesia, Kawasan Industri Pulogadung
JI. Rawa Gelam IV No. 9, Jakarta 13930
Tel: (62) 21 4682-1088
Fax: (62) 21 461-0206
crm@periplus.co.id
www.periplus.com

20 19 18 17
10 9 8 7 6 5 4 3 2 1

Printed in China   1703RR

ABOUT TUTTLE
"Books to Span the East and West"

Our core mission at Tuttle Publishing is to create books which bring people together one page at a time. Tuttle was founded in 1832 in the small New England town of Rutland, Vermont (USA). Our fundamental values remain as strong today as they were then—to publish best-in-class books informing the English-speaking world about the countries and peoples of Asia. The world has become a smaller place today and Asia's economic, cultural and political influence has expanded, yet the need for meaningful dialogue and information about this diverse region has never been greater. Since 1948, Tuttle has been a leader in publishing books on the cultures, arts, cuisines, languages and literatures of Asia. Our authors and photographers have won numerous awards and Tuttle has published thousands of books on subjects ranging from martial arts to paper crafts. We welcome you to explore the wealth of information available on Asia at **www.tuttlepublishing.com**.